Fight Back

A 30 Day Woman's Guide to Praying For Your Husband

Table of Contents

Preface

A typical morning for me starts at 5 o'clock in the morning and consists of something hot, something soothing for the soul. From oolong and dandelion tea, to mint or detox tea, and coffee of course for 'that' kind of morning. A hot cup of tea feels like a big hug to me. Of course my love language is physical touch, acts of service running a close second! In other words, bring me a hot cup of tea in a really cute cup and instantly I am feeling relaxed and thankful. True Story! Snacks of course accompany me depending on my mood. Sometimes waking up is not easy for me so a banana and almonds is needed for energy.

One morning I woke up and began to pray over my family. The Holy Spirit told me to pray over my husband and prophesy over him for 30 days. He then instructed me to invite other women to do the same through *Facebook.* I felt this was the leading of the Lord. He spoke and then confirmed what He was speaking to me by manifesting His presence. It was an AMEN from me.

There were instructions that I needed to follow. The Lord did not want me to write out a devotional for you to read and repeat. He wanted me to exhort you to pray to Him *yourself* and hear His instruction regarding *your* husband.

This 30-day prayer guide will draw you closer to the Lord and your husband will be blessed by the overflow. Prayer has to be an ongoing discipline. Sometimes you will have opportunities to pray more passionately for your marriage than usual. My husband was active duty Air Force for 24 years. I prayed more fervently for his safety and peace of mind in a way that I did not typically pray when he was at home and not living in a war zone. I am grateful to this day that the Lord honored my prayers for my husband. John 7:38 says, 'He that believeth on me, as the scripture hath said, out of his belly shall flow rivers of living water.'

Okay ladies let's do this. Get your hot tea and invite the Holy Spirit in so that your communion with Him is intimate.

Dear Sister girl,

Accept your role. Whether you are headed to divorce court or not, accept your role because you are still married. If you are separated, the divorce is not final, accept your role. Is he incarcerated? Yep, you got it, accept your role.

Rest assured that when God designed man and woman there were absolutely without a shadow of a doubt no mistakes. As the helpmeet/Ezer Kenegdo you have the mental capacity to be alert and walk in pristine discernment that is right for your husband. God said, 'It is not good that the man should be alone; I will make him a help meet for him' (Genesis 2:18). A *wise* husband will listen to his wife as she gently and wisely cautions her man of impending danger or issues that are ahead. If your husband is not a wise man it may be because of many reasons. Maybe he is not a believer, maybe he has issues of the heart, maybe he had a bad experience with church. Whatever it is, he won't listen if you are harsh so bring it in and calm it down. 'As a jewel of gold in a swine's snout, so is a fair woman which is without discretion.' Underline that in your Bible under Proverbs 11:22. Remember, these 30 days are going to be interactive so be sure to have pen and Bible in hand.

It is very hard for a helpmeet/Ezer Kenegdo to feel free when the person she is called to help will not submit to the Holy Spirit that speaks through her. She will begin to shut down and become callous in different ways. It is called a coping mechanism.

Pray that your husband will trust you and fear God enough to accept your role as a TYPE of Holy Spirit as you submit to his role as a TYPE of Christ. Remember Proverbs 11:22 and learn what discretion means. As a matter of fact, stop and look it up in the dictionary and write the definition on this line.

_____

_____

Now, if you have become callous, go QUICKLY and receive wise counsel. If you need healing in your soul from the battle wounds of marriage, get counsel. Your husband needs you, he may not realize it, especially if his heart issues are front and center; however, the acceptance of your role will make a big difference! Pray for him! #FightBack

Titus 2 Matters,
Alaine

Day 1 - Prophecy the Word of God

Today's Date:

Lay hands on your husband and pray. Prophesy the Word of God over him. Bless him with your affirmations of how much of a blessing he is to you, the children and the community. To prophesy means to speak the heart of God over your husband, to speak into what you see regarding his future even if you don't see it today. This is where Hebrews 11:1 comes into play. Look that reference up.

By prophesying over your husband, you are establishing divine government. If you don't do what you are supposed to do he won't either! By prophesying over your husband for 30 days you will have contractions. Contractions? Yes! You will experience some emotional pain. You may remember 'that thing' he did that hurt you.

You may remember that betrayal, that lie, and that abuse. Breathe, invite the Ruach HaKodesh (Hebrew for Holy Spirit) in to speak to your spirit so that you can adjust your soul, mind, will and emotions. Keep pushing, praying over your husband. You CANNOT give him what is NOT in you, so get your daily bread through prayer and allow your husbands spirit to feast off what you collect in your morning worship.

Ask the Lord to speak to you through dreams and visions concerning your husband or your certain someone. Be prepared for that prayer to be answered. The Lord speaks through prayers. Write the prayer down soon after you wake up or you may forget it.

Day 1 Journaling
#FightBack

_____
_____
_____
_____
_____
_____
_____
_____
_____
_____
_____
_____
_____
_____
_____
_____
_____
_____
_____
_____
_____

Day 2 - Consistency

Today's Date:

Consistency. Even though he may fall short in areas of his life, speak over him. Speak truth over him. The truth is the scripture. Choose 2 or 3 scriptures that you want to see manifested in his life and journal it. Pray the scripture as if he is already walking in the truth. If he's not kind, lay your hands on him and thank God for his kindness. If he's not in the Word, thank the Lord for his hunger and thirst for righteousness.

Faith! Operate in the dimension of faith! NOW 'faith is the substance of things hoped for and the evidence of things not seen!' That verse is found in Hebrews 11:1. Take a moment and highlight it in your Bible. Once highlighted, pray that over your life.

Ready? Go!

Day 2 Journaling
#FightBack

_____

_____

_____

_____

_____

_____

_____

_____

_____

_____

_____

_____

_____

_____

_____

_____

_____

_____

_____

_____

_____

_____

Day 3 - Don't be Weary

Today's Date:

Do not become weary in praying over your husband and stop. That will make the devil and his cousins really happy. There cannot be a honeymoon stage regarding prayer. Prayer is life and breath. These prayers for your husband are not coming from a book or a manual. These prayers are coming from your belly (spirit). It is what YOU put in your belly that will cause growth in your man because he will be blessed from the overflow. Find a scripture about prayer and write it in your day 3 journal.

Memorize the scripture because the Word of God is a sword.

Day 3 Journal
#FightBack

_____

_____

_____

_____

_____

_____

_____

_____

_____

_____

_____

_____

_____

_____

_____

_____

_____

_____

_____

_____

_____

_____

Day 4 - He Will Boast

Today's Date:

Good morning! Proverbs 31:28 says, 'Her children arise up, and call her blessed; her husband also, and he praiseth her.' Praiseth means to be boastful, to be commended, be made praiseworthy, to shine God's favor. Did you hear what the Lord just said? He said YOUR husband will BOAST about YOU! He will tell all how God's favor is on you. He will commend you. To commend means to entrust or to trust. YOUR husband is supposed to trust you. YOU! The question is, does your husband trust you? If not, what is your plan to rebuild that structure? Write your goals and write down the steps needed to make it happen. We are Hebrew women, everything we do is a verb.

If your husband is NOT boasting and praising you, why isn't he? Pray over your man today. The prayers that come from your spirit after you connect with the Holy Spirit is a balm. Your prayers are going to be a healing agent. Wait for it. Consistency!

The ONLY way your husband will be able to trust you is if you are consistent. Let me backup. You are HIS good thing. Let's define "a good thing" according to the Strong's Concordance

1. pleasant, agreeable (to the senses)
2. pleasant (to the higher nature)
3. good, excellent (of its kind)
4. rich, valuable in estimation
5. appropriate, becoming (flattering, attractive, lovely), better
6. glad, happy, prosperous (of man's sensuous nature)

7. good understanding (of man's intellectual nature)
8. good, right (ethical)

You see? If you are operating as HIS "good thing" then the above description will be seen by YOUR husband and what will happen? He will praise you. Let's look at the word "favor" because the Lord says your husband will obtain favor of the Lord. It means, pleasure or delight and comes from the root word, *ratsah* which means to be pleased with. So, in other words because YOU are operating in numbers 1-8 your husband will be pleased and bless you. The Lord will be *delighted* in him!!! Why?

Because you birthed him into his rightful place through prayer. You made HIM better!! You made HIM to be known in the "gate" we will talk about that tomorrow. If your husband is not doing right by God, what are you doing spiritually to get information from the Lord on what to do next? The LORD WILL speak to you in prayer and fasting. Yep, if things are hard and you feel weary, it is time for you to fast.

Day 4 Journaling
#FightBack

_____

_____

_____

_____

_____

_____

_____

_____

_____

_____

_____

_____

_____

_____

_____

_____

_____

_____

_____

_____

_____

_____

Day 5 - Your Dreams

Today's Date:

Pay attention to "your" dreams during these days of deliberately praying over your husband. Your dreams are a direct link to the realm of the spirit if they are not coming from your soulish nature. A dream from the soul is a carryover dream regarding anything you have been worrying about or anything that affects your thoughts during the day. When you have dreams be sure to get dream interpretation. Don't ignore the voice of God in the realm of the spirit. *Do not* allow the enemy to divide and conquer during this time. The fact that you are speaking life over your husband or significant other consistently is a *threat* to the demonic realm. Ladies, BE SOBER, BE VIGILANT! PRAY!

Write down 1 Peter 5:8 in your journal and memorize it.

If you do not understand spiritual warfare you need to search it out, do a Google search or get with someone in your circle who can explain and teach the concept. Let me get you started. Turn to Ephesians 6:12 in your Bible and highlight it if you haven't already. Basically, spiritual warfare is an invisible fight with fallen angels called demons. Demons like to aggravate the lives of Christians to cause defeat. So, you see, your fight is not with your husband. It is with fallen angels that seek to destroy your union. If you are not fighting with demons then pay attention to the manifestation of the unpleasant human nature known as the flesh. You can go to Galatians 5:19-26 in your Bible to understand what people do when they are giving in to their human nature. Regarding spiritual warfare, if you do not understand that you are in a spiritual war, then you may be losing and are completely unaware.

Hosea 4:6 says, 'My people are being destroyed because they don't know me. Since your priests refuse to know me, I refuse to recognize you as my priests. Since you have forgotten the laws of your God, I will forget to bless your children.'

Some of you may be struggling to pray for your husband because he is not "acting" like you want him to act; perhaps he is not receiving like you want him to receive you and the Word. Do not be moved by it AT ALL!! It is a distraction, a smoke screen. Stay in the realm of the spirit and be slow to speak!!! If you argue back or if you play into the smoke screen on any level, you get sucked back in and the battle in your mind will be more of the same.

Listen, do not pay attention to what you see on the outside. Pay attention to what you see in the spirit when you pray, dream, meditate and soak in the presence of the Lord. Your emotions cannot be trusted. We all have emotions and emotions are not bad in and of themselves. Emotions help us gage situations and circumstances. At times emotions cannot be trusted because they don't often speak to what is true. Emotions are often predicated off of perceptions and when the perception changes then the emotion changes. So, respect your emotions but trust the Word of the Lord.

Day 5 Journal
#FightBack

_____

_____

_____

_____

_____

_____

_____

_____

_____

_____

_____

_____

_____

_____

_____

_____

_____

_____

_____

_____

_____

Day 6 - Christ is the Center

Today's Date:

   Check to make sure that Christ is at the center of your marriage. I have a question. Do you and your husband pray and plan together? Have you written your financial, educational, business, or leisure plan together? How are you building your house? Psalm 127:1 from God's Word Translations says, "If the Lord does not build the house, it is useless for the builders to work on it." Why? Because the Lord is not at the center. Everything you say and do must align with the Word of God or must come from the words of wisdom and knowledge that God speaks to your spirit. Building a home without a blueprint leads to disaster. Spending money without a budget does not create a good steward over the money that the Lord has allowed you to make. Living from week to week without a calendar is not a well planned out week. Praying invites the Lord into your planning and puts Him at the center of your marriage. Open your Bible to John 15:5 and memorize that verse.

   'In all of your ways acknowledge Him and He will direct your path.' Underline that in your Bible. You can find it in Proverbs 3:6. Prophesy and speak that over yourself.

   The path He tells us to take may not be comfortable for our habits. We must lay our lives down for others. I did not say lay down and be abused. I said let the Lord direct you and what He says, you must do. The. End. He is a jealous God, do not arouse His righteous indignation.

   Your husband feeds off your obedience to Yah. Your words, your touch, your body, your love, your food, your domestic and professional qualities etc., are all things that feed your husband when done in excellence. Why?

Because you are his good thang! So, do not blaspheme the Word of God. Read Titus 2:3-5 for understanding.

If your weapons are not spiritual, then you are not winning. You may think you are, but according the scripture, strongholds can only be pulled down spiritually. 2 Corinthians 10:4 is the reference and as always, highlight that in your Bible and memorize it. Don't let your accuser use you to carry out his assignment.

Day 6 Journaling
#FightBack

_____

_____

_____

_____

_____

_____

_____

_____

_____

_____

_____

_____

_____

_____

_____

_____

_____

_____

_____

_____

_____

_____

Day 7 - Pay Attention

Today's Date:

Okay ladies, do not let your guard down! Pray for that man! Love him beyond the besetting sin that ensnares him just like Hebrews 12:1 declares. Love crushes the stoniest heart! Selah...

Watch your tone today. Watch your facial expressions. A meek spirit goes a long way!

Okay, so he may still not be "acting" like you want him to. Maybe he is not receiving like you want him to receive. Do not be moved by it AT ALL!! It is a distraction, a smoke screen. Stay in the realm of the spirit and press your lips together! Turn to Romans 3:10 and decide who is perfect.

If things are going well for you in your marriage right now, great! Press on my sister.

Day 7 Journaling
#FightBack

_____

_____

_____

_____

_____

_____

_____

_____

_____

_____

_____

_____

_____

_____

_____

_____

_____

_____

_____

_____

_____

_____

_____

Day 8 – Command His Day

Good morning! Continue to command your husband's day!

Job 38:12 says, 'Hast thou commanded (commission, give orders, charge, appoint) the morning (the 4th watch which is the end of the night, when the sun begins to break through) since thy days; and caused the dayspring to know his place. (*Parentheses are mine for emphasis)

WHOA!! Did y'all catch that? You can commission and give orders to your husband's day early in the morning. The 4th watch of the night is between 3AM and 6AM.

Do you see the power of your words in Job 38:12? Proverbs 18:21 reminds us that, 'Life and death is in the power of the tongue and them that love it will eat the fruit there of.'Remember that word power means yad (hand, strength, power).

So, you see my sisters, when you command his day you have the power to strengthen his hand with your words. MY!! SAVIOR!! Mmm! This is soooo good! #FightBack

You may feel like your husband is not establishing goals and dreams for the family; ask the Holy Spirit why and keep your heart open to receive the truth.

Underline Proverbs 31:11 in your Bible and memorize it. The scripture says, 'The heart of her husband doth safely trust in her, so that he shall have no need of spoil.' The same scripture in the New Living

Translation reads, 'Her husband can trust her, and she will greatly enrich his life.'

Remember, you are his *"good thang"* and you cause him to obtain favor. I get that some husbands have dealt treacherously with you. Know this, you were not created to follow abuse. #FightBack using wisdom, help from the laws of the land, prayer, and godly counsel.

Day 8 Journaling
#FightBack

_____

_____

_____

_____

_____

_____

_____

_____

_____

_____

_____

_____

_____

_____

_____

_____

_____

_____

_____

_____

_____

_____

_____

_____

Day 9 - A Wife's Response

Today's Date:

How are you responding to your husband's small requests?

If you have a strong personality, it may be hard to humble yourself. Here is the thing, the smallest resemblance of opposition toward your husband is enough to discourage him, making him feel like a castrated, muted yes man that you can continue to control. Dear lady, Stop it.

When your husband makes a small request and you fail to catch it and honor that thing, it will discourage him from leading. I hear in my spirit that some are saying, "the smallest request?" Yes, the smallest request. I also hear that some of you women do not hear the request because you don't hear his voice. Why? Subconscious dishonor. Take time to hear your husband's words and honor what he is not saying through discernment. Win back his trust. Don't try to get your way. Win back his trust. "The smallest request."

Day 9 Journaling
#FightBack

_____
_____
_____
_____
_____
_____
_____
_____
_____
_____
_____
_____
_____
_____
_____
_____
_____
_____
_____
_____
_____

Day 10 - Loyalty and Support

Today's Date:

Loyalty and Support!

Fit into your husband's plan. If you are a foolish wife, you will crush your husband's spirit and become rotten to his bones. Here is what the scripture says, 'A virtuous woman *is* a crown to her husband: but she that maketh ashamed *is* as rottenness in his bones.' Look up that verse and underline that verse in your Bible and memorize it for prayer.

I remember when my husband was diagnosed with high blood pressure. We lived in Germany and I told my spiritual mom what the doctors said. She responded with this, "You've got to fit into your husband's plan." She went on to say that I had to learn about the condition and align our (even though it was "his" diagnosis, it was our issue.) diet, and lifestyle after the pursuit of healing. That was called fitting into his plan for getting that BP under control.

Those words have stuck with me. When my husband deployed I was called to fit into his plan and not complain. When he went back to school I had to fit into his plan. His life became mine and he needed loyalty and support. Recently, my husband has told me he is planning on going back to school. I must fit into his plan because his schooling will advance his purpose for the Kingdom of God.

Do you know your husband's purpose? Goals? Dreams? Do you know how he feels about how you keep the home and raise the children? What are his pet peeves? Are you loyal and supportive? Are you fitting into his plan? When you know these things, you offend the enemy.

Day 10 Journaling
#FightBack

_____

_____

_____

_____

_____

_____

_____

_____

_____

_____

_____

_____

_____

_____

_____

_____

_____

_____

_____

_____

_____

Day 11 - Your Irritations

Today's Date:

Your irritations.

IRRITATION: the state of feeling annoyed, impatient, or angry.

SYNONYMS FOR IRRITATION: annoyance, exasperation, indignation, impatience, displeasure, anger, rage, wrath, aggravation.

Patience? Well, what does THAT look like? (chuckling internally) To be patient means to be tolerant. Ladies, tolerating things means that you may suffer just a bit and carry the burden until change comes. We should expect patience to be the hard work we usually find it to be.

Ohhhhh myyyy! Did you hear that ladies? Your husband (friends, family, co-workers, church members etc.) is going to cause an irritation or an annoyance within your soul. BUT, your work is to tolerate the situation, check your motive and submit to the Lord. Check. Your. Motive. Why are you irritated? Typically, it is because we are not getting our own way and we do not want to tolerate his flaws, his immaturity, his lack, his broken promises, HIS_____(fill in the blank).

1 Corinthians 13:5 reminds us that, 'Love is not rude, it is not selfish, and it cannot be made angry easily. Love does not remember wrongs done against it.' Patience is a weapon!

Day 11 Journaling
#FightBack

_____

_____

_____

_____

_____

_____

_____

_____

_____

_____

_____

_____

_____

_____

_____

_____

_____

_____

_____

_____

_____

_____

Day 12 - Caution

Today's Date:

Pause when you see a caution regarding your husband.

If your husband does not listen to your wisdom or to your cautions, be confident that God is going to get the glory. The End! You yelling and repeating yourself will not change your husband. You belittling him and talking about him to your sista's will not change him. It hasn't, and it won't. Have faith that you will learn in the valley.

Let me say it another way. As the Ezer, "sometimes" you can see the foxes in the vineyard. You see clearly but your husband may not. You see the red flashing lights, the bell is ringing, the flag is being waved...but he does not discern. What then? If we get angry, talk back, display an attitude, pucker our lips, withhold sex, disrespect his lack of discernment...we are OUT. OF. ORDER!

Repeat. We cannot change our husbands. When you try to push your way even if it is right, we run the risk of damaging God's child. OUCH! DON'T DO IT!! If that man will not listen to God, what makes you think he will listen to you? I'm just saying! You cannot change him, it is the work of the Holy Spirit. Step away from the temptation to operate in #witchcraft and allow that man to be subdued by the Holy Ghost!

Let that man GO! Release him to the Lord. Intercede for his wisdom to be awakened. Ask the Lord to use someone else to speak into his spirit and regulate his soul. Keep quiet and PRAY! #FightBack

When you find yourself stuck in the whirlwind of discouragement and negative emotions... Go to God with praise music, worship His character and promises and pray. If that does not work, go and seek wise counsel. Wise. Counsel. Not your wounded friend. There is a difference between counsel and wise counsel!

Day 12 Journaling
#FightBack

Day 13 - Discouragement

Today's Date:

Discouragement Exposes Your Weaknesses.

Woooo Sa! Yep, your response to disappointments and discouragement within your marriage will expose your real character. It is actually a pop quiz of your maturity level. What do you do when pressure and pain encompasses your heart and mind?

James 1:3-6 says, 'You know that under pressure, your faith-life is forced into the open and shows its true colors. So, don't try to get out of anything prematurely. Let it do its work so you become mature and well-developed, not deficient in any way. If you don't know what you're doing, pray to the Father. He loves to help. You'll get his help and won't be condemned when you ask for it. Ask boldly, with belief, and without a second thought.'

PRESS! Press into the truth of the Word and worship until your mind is transformed.

Day 13 Journaling
#FightBack

Day 14 - The Honeymoon Stage

Today's Date:

The Honeymoon Stage is...well...just keep reading.

We have all heard of the honeymoon stage of a relationship. That is when the passion is most intense, adrenaline runs deep and your desire to be with your spouse is heavy (cue harp music).

(Cue the sound of the needle scratching a vinyl record)

Let's face it, your honeymoon stage of praying for your spouse may be subsiding and for some of you it never happened. You may be getting bored with the idea of marriage, your passion may be decreasing, the adrenaline may be gone, the dirty laundry of his soul may be causing you grief and these early morning wake up calls may be kicking your tail.

(Cue boxing ring bell indicating the next round)

Don't succumb to the false notions of prayer. Prayer is not always filled with excitement. Prayer is not always filled with the "feeling" that the Lord is hovering like a cloud and fire. Nothing is meant to be on 10 all the time. There cannot be an attention deficit of hyperactivity in prayer all the time. Don't be bamboozled.

Your obedience to the Lord is key! Praying the Word because it will not return void is the key. Keeping in step with kavanah is key. The honeymoon stage lasting forever is not a reality. After the honeymoon it is time to put in some work!

We just went to the next level of maturity in praying over our husbands. This is not about a feeling; it is okay if the honeymoon of this 30 days is gone. PRESS!

Be clear-minded and alert. Your opponent, the devil, is prowling around like a roaring lion, looking for someone to devour. You can find that verse in 1 Peter 5:8.

Day 14 Journal
#FightBack

_____

_____

_____

_____

_____

_____

_____

_____

_____

_____

_____

_____

_____

_____

_____

_____

_____

_____

_____

_____

_____

Day 15 - A Word from Your Pastor

Today's Date:

Good MORNING!

Do you have a church home? If you do, great! If you do not, you have a problem. Many think that being a member of the local church is unnecessary. What is the condition of your spirit? Are you easily offended? Are you bitter? Would you rather not deal with people? Are you critical? If so, you should consider getting some inner healing and maybe even some professional counseling.

There is nothing wrong with professional counseling; I am an advocate for it. Your heart issues have cut you off from people. 1 John 1:5-7 says, 'This is the message we heard from Christ and are reporting to you: God is light, and there isn't any darkness in Him.' If we say, "We have a relationship with God" and yet live in the dark, we're lying. We aren't being truthful. But if we live in the light in the same way that God is in the light, we have a relationship with each other. And the blood of his Son Jesus cleanses us from every sin. In other words, fellowship with God means fellowship with people.' Do you see that in the scripture?

Your pastor prepares a message for you on a weekly basis. It is a part of your daily bread! The next message you hear from your pastor will be what you need to pray over and prophesy to your husband in prayer. Hallelujah! I feel the Holy Ghost. Be prepared to hear specifically from the Lord as your pastor brings the word!

Day 15 Journaling
#FightBack

_____

_____

_____

_____

_____

_____

_____

_____

_____

_____

_____

_____

_____

_____

_____

_____

_____

_____

_____

_____

_____

_____

Day 16 - Do Not Compare

Today's Date:

Do not compare. Period!

Galatians 6:4 says, 'Don't compare yourself with others. Just look at your own work to see if you have done anything to be proud of. You must each accept the responsibilities that are yours.'

Deception will cause you to think that her (points to the couple across the church) marriage looks so good and that they are so happy. Deception will turn into jealousy and it will be all because of your perception. Perceptions, by the way can be lies.

Marriage has highs and lows. Husbands (and wives, I gotta keep this balanced - lol) are not perfect. We are all full of flaws (cue crucifixion graphic) therefore, we need a Savior.

'Godliness with contentment is great gain. For we brought nothing into this world, and it is certain we can carry nothing out. And having food and raiment let us be therewith content.' Underline I Timothy 6:6–8 in your Bible.

Contentment in this verse means, "sufficiency of the necessities of life." (read that again) A traditional list of immediate "basic needs" is found in the Maslow's hierarchy of needs model. Check that out in *Google*.

Sooo...my sisters if you have the basic necessities of life, you are doing well!! Be okay, with that. Do not covet another person's relationship because you do not know what they went through to bare that fruit; do not compare your relationship with another. Do not compare your husband to another. No relationship is perfect, not mine and not yours. We must die to comparison.

Day 16 Journal
#FightBack

Day 17 - Forgive

Today's Date:

Forgive! I know, we have heard that a million times.

If you refuse to humble yourself and admit your personal failures regarding your marriage and your attitude toward your man, you will most likely cause his heart to grow hard toward yours.

Maybe you snapped at him, maybe you used sarcasm, maybe you rolled your eyes, maybe you raised your volume because he raised his volume, maybe your tone was wrong, etc. That leaven can cause a chasm in the marriage. Those foxes over time can cause distance in the marriage. Ask for forgiveness even if he "started" it.

If at any time you feel like you do not want to apologize for your part in the wrong - pride is lurking. When we did not do anything wrong and the Holy Spirit says to apologize and pride kicks in - we need to be humbled.

Listen, personal character flaws can damage your union. Judge your attitude as well as your actions and determine what your verbal and nonverbal communication is telling your husband. Do you really want to be humbled? Ask him to share the hurts that *you* have infected his soul with. Ouch! When he musters up enough courage to share with you how he feels, it will behoove you to take it and hush. Tell him "thank you" for sharing and then go and processes it with the Holy Ghost, a trusted friend or professional.

No justification needed here, this is all about humbling yourself. Listen to your spouse! Ask for forgiveness when you have done wrong and accept God's grace to bring complete reformation to the compromising actions and attitudes that you house.

'If I regard iniquity in my heart, the Lord will not hear me' is what Psalm 66:18 says. 'Blessed are the peacemakers, for they will be called children of God' comes from Matthew 5:9. Apologize!

Day 17 Journaling
#FightBack

_____
_____
_____
_____
_____
_____
_____
_____
_____
_____
_____
_____
_____
_____
_____
_____
_____
_____
_____
_____
_____
_____
_____
_____

Day 18 - Restitution

Today's Date:

Restitution!

Restitution. What is restitution? Glad you asked. "Restitution is the act of making up for damages or harm" according to Merriam-Webster.

When you do or say something that brings pain to your spouse, a sincere apology is necessary. Sometimes, after the apology, restitution is necessary. What act of service can you do to restore your husband? Friend? Co-worker? Child? Enemy? What do they need from you as a salve of restoration? Have you ever asked?

'Make allowance for each other's faults and forgive anyone who offends you. Remember, the Lord forgave you, so you must forgive others. Above all, clothe yourselves with love, which binds us all together in perfect harmony' Colossians 3:13-14 (NLT). Whew, now that is plain. No excuses can be interjected here. No conjunctions here ladies. Maybe a foot washing is needed. Humble yourself and do something to bring restitution. Find out what they need for restoration and do it. Restitution is a weapon.

Day 18 Journaling
#FightBack

_____

_____

_____

_____

_____

_____

_____

_____

_____

_____

_____

_____

_____

_____

_____

_____

_____

_____

_____

Day 19 - Demonic Cycles

Today's Date:

Pray Against Demonic Cycles because they are real!

Let's read Deuteronomy 7:1-6 because some of us have "ites" in our lives. Those "ites" are preventing us from getting into the land God promised us. Have you ever progressed only to find that you are right back where you started? Have you ever found yourself in a cycle? You may have an "ites" that are overpowering your victory.

Deuteronomy 7:1-6 says:

> When the Lord your God brings you into the land you are entering to possess and drives out before you many nations—the Hittites, Girgashites, Amorites, Canaanites, Perizzites, Hivites and Jebusites, seven nations larger and stronger than you— 2 and when the Lord your God has delivered them over to you and you have defeated them, then you must destroy them totally. Make no treaty with them and show them no mercy. 3 Do not intermarry with them. Do not give your daughters to their sons or take their daughters for your sons, 4 for they will turn your children away from following me to serve other gods, and the Lord's anger will burn against you and will quickly destroy you. 5 This is what you are to do to them: Break down their altars, smash their sacred stones, cut down their Asherah poles and burn their idols in the fire. 6 For you are a people holy to the Lord your God. The Lord your God has chosen you out of all the people on the face of the earth to be his people, his treasured possession.

Patterns, habits and cycles that stop growth need to be dealt with in the most no-nonsense manner! Study how each of those "ites" manifest and gain victory. Write a list of bad cycles in your marriage. Find a scripture to counter the cycle and pray it over your marriage.

I have given you the authority to trample snakes and scorpions and to destroy the enemy's power. Nothing will hurt you' underline that in your Bible in Luke 10:19.

Day 19 Journaling
#FightBack

_____

_____

_____

_____

_____

_____

_____

_____

_____

_____

_____

_____

_____

_____

_____

_____

_____

_____

_____

_____

_____

Day 20 - Finish Strong

Today's Date:

Finish Strong!! Strength is your portion when you are weak.

Ecclesiastes 7:8 from the ESV says, 'Better is the end of a thing than its beginning, and the patient in spirit is better than the proud in spirit.'

WHOA! Read this commentary from The Bible Illustrator, "The fruit is better than the blossom; the reaping is better than the sowing; the enjoyment than the reaping; the second stage of a journey to the happy home is better than the first; the home itself than all; the victory is better than the march and the battle; the reward is better than the course of service; the ending in the highest improvement of means is better than being put at first in possession of them."

You see what I am saying? The enemy does not care if we start a thing, he cares if we finish strong! This is the part in the journey that you may feel weary, bored, or underappreciated etc. This is the time to shift into a higher gear! Finish strong! Do this as unto the Lord!

Day 20 Journaling
#FightBack

_____

_____

_____

_____

_____

_____

_____

_____

_____

_____

_____

_____

_____

_____

_____

_____

_____

_____

_____

_____

_____

Day 21 - Don't Push the Issue

Today's Date:

Don't push the issue. Please don't. Let it go.

Girlfriend, once you have brought something to his attention and you have communicated clearly… do not push the issue. Nagging never works. You think it is eventually going to work but really, he may be doing whatever it is he needs to do to get some peace of mind. Don't believe me? Proverbs 27:15-16 says, 'A quarrelsome wife is as annoying as constant dripping on a rainy day. Stopping her complaints is like trying to stop the wind or trying to hold something with greased hands.' Pushing the issue makes him feel like you are nagging or quarrelsome. To be quarrelsome simply means to be combative, cantankerous and disagreeable. Taking the issue to your prayer closet and asking the Lord to open the doorway of utterance so that you can revisit the issue is what a wise woman does. Don't push the issue.

Never approach an issue in the height of your emotions. Never ever do that! It only leads to more chaos. Give yourself a few days to settle down and hear clearly. I repeat, hear clearly… from the Lord. And let me just say this to those of you who do not address things when the Lord opens the door… Let's call that group of women, "stuffers". Stuffing is the other extreme of pushing an issue. Both result in damaged emotions and crushed spirits.

'Fear of the Lord is the foundation of wisdom. Knowledge of the Holy One results in good judgment. Wisdom will multiply your days and add years to your life. If you become wise, you will be the one to benefit. If you scorn wisdom, you will be the one to suffer' that's Proverbs 9:10-12 from the New Living Translation. I think you may want to study that out for revelation knowledge.

If you have already brought it to his attention, do not press the issue until the Lord opens the opportunity! It will take self-control. Do not stuff the issue when the Lord opens the opportunity! It's called courage. Do not pray that a situation will get better and stay in an abusive situation. That is called foolishness. You are not called to be abused. So, #FightBack if you are in a domestic violence or sexual assault situation. As a matter of fact, you can call *The National Domestic Violence Hotline,* advocates are available 24/7 at 1-800-799-SAFE (7233) in more than 200 languages. All calls are free and confidential. If you are in a sexually abusive situation, call 800- 656-HOPE (4673) to be connected with a trained staff member from a sexual assault service provider in your area.

Day 21 Journaling
#FightBack

_____

_____

_____

_____

_____

_____

_____

_____

_____

_____

_____

_____

_____

_____

_____

_____

_____

_____

_____

_____

Day 22 - Roll Call

Today's Date:

Roll Call! You are still fighting back aren't you?

Proverbs 27:17 says, 'Iron sharpens iron, and one man sharpens another.'

Today isn't going to be geared toward your husband. Instead, let's talk about you.

In the *Journal of Biblical Literature* by Ronald L. Giese Jr. he writes, "The above scripture likens the interaction between two faithful friends who are seeking the improvement of one another to the sharpening of an iron stone or other iron tool against an iron sharpener. The analogy is even clearer in the Hebrew, for the second half of the verse can be translated as "one man sharpens the face of another." Just as a man might sharpen the face of his sword against a sharpening iron to make it more suitable for combat, so does a faithful friend equip his friend for success by constructive criticism."

WOW! Roll call! Who is still being faithful to praying for your husband, friend, or significant other? Are you continuing to sharpen your spouse? Have you lost your zeal? Your commitment? Who keeps YOU sharpened?

Are you one who sharpens others? In this walk we must ALL have accountability! We must all be sharpened, corrected, instructed, even rebuked. Who are you vulnerable with? Who is vulnerable with you?

Let us know if you are continuing in your 30 days of faithful prayer over your boo by going to our *Facebook* page #AlaineCoaches and leave a message. Let us know what 30 days of prayer is doing for you.

Day 22 Journal
#FightBack

_____

_____

_____

_____

_____

_____

_____

_____

_____

_____

_____

_____

_____

_____

_____

_____

_____

_____

_____

Day 23 - Identify Emotions

Today's Date:

Identify the emotion and process!

As a human you have been given emotions, so embrace them. Embrace all emotions painful and joyous because they are yours. Give honor to your emotions because they are there. Recognize you are feeling an emotion whether positive or negative. Give the emotion a name such as disgust, anger, fear, sadness etc. and then ask yourself 'why' questions up to 5 times after identifying an emotion. This will help you process the emotion.

For example, you feel frustration (which is a nice word for anger) because hubby does something. Tell yourself how you feel. I feel disrespected. Then ask yourself why? Why do I feel disrespected? Then answer (we are processing) why you feel disrespected. I feel disrespected because he knows I've been under the weather, he could have gotten dinner. Next why. Why didn't you make arrangements for him to pick up a chicken from Walmart? The answer may be, "Why do I have to think of everything?" Third why question. Are you really thinking of *everything*? The answer is, "no". Fourth why question. So then why do you feel disrespected? The answer may be because you want him to think like you and it is not going to happen.

Matthew 7:7 says, 'Ask, and it shall be given you; seek, and ye shall find; knock, and it shall be opened unto you.' If God expects us to ask, then why wouldn't our husbands require maturity from us? If God expects us to seek, then why not seek out the hidden things of the heart to get to a place of emotional intelligence.

Identify the emotion and process! You may discover selfish motives that are rooted in pride or you may discover that your husband is a bit selfish and needs self-examination. Proceed with wisdom.

Day 23 Journaling
#FightBack

_____

_____

_____

_____

_____

_____

_____

_____

_____

_____

_____

_____

_____

_____

_____

_____

_____

_____

_____

_____

_____

_____

_____

Day 24 - Prudence is a Weapon

Today's Date:

Prudence is a weapon, no doubt!

'House and riches are the inheritance of fathers: and a prudent wife is from the Lord" underline that in your Bible, Proverbs 19:14.

Prudent? What does that mean? It means to be wise or to have insight. Hmmmm...let's make this a bit more practical.

Have you ever heard someone's mother say, "If you do not have anything nice to say, do not say anything at all?" Sometimes it is better to say nothing at all than to say anything, that is called prudence. A prudent woman is wise when she handles day to day matters.

WHOA!! That has nothing to do with operating in our emotions. Prudence will cause a Woman of God to walk in a way that is pleasing to the Lord Jesus Christ. Prudence will cause a Woman of God to know how to minister to her husband's weaknesses. Prudence is a wise woman. Prudence is a discerning woman, a self-controlled woman.

WHOA! WHOA! WHOA! I feel like this one word can be taught for the next 3 days! Let's pray for prudence in our lives. Let's pray that we will be a blessing of prudence in our husband's life. Why? Because the scripture says a prudent wife comes from the LORD! Prudence is a weapon!

Day 24 Journaling
#FightBack

_____
_____
_____
_____
_____
_____
_____
_____
_____
_____
_____
_____
_____
_____
_____
_____
_____
_____
_____
_____

Day 25 - Proverbs 31:30

Today's Date:

Proverbs 31:30 from the Easy Standard Version of the Bible says, 'Charm is deceitful, and beauty is vain, but a woman who fears the Lord is to be praised.'

'But a woman who fears the Lord SHALL be praised!' Praised for her constant pouring out. Praised for her continual sacrificial offerings. Praised for orchestrating the rhythm of her home. Praised for going to bed last and rising early. Praised for training her children and loving her husband. Praised for making huge mistakes and repenting. Praised for seeking the Lord when her heart is full of joy and full of pain. WOW!

I remember when my children were younger, my body and my mind would be exhausted from chores, child rearing, errands etc. Some days I wondered if *anyone* noticed my efforts. Some days I felt discouraged. But the scripture says that because we fear the Lord we are worthy to be praised! Do you fear the Lord? You are worthy to be praised. So, I praise you!

'Her husband's life is full of joy, for his heart can safely trust in her' is what Proverbs 31:11says. When your husband trusts you, he will eat from your hand. 'She will do him good and not evil all the days of her life', we should always remember this from Proverbs 31:12. I encourage you to go a little deeper into this scripture and read some commentaries, study the scripture for yourself and then hide it in your heart.

If you didn't know, please know that this woman is worthy to be praised! Do not compare yourself to this woman. This woman is you! You are a work in progress. God's sanctification process is still processing. Keep praying for your husband. Make these last five days count. I'm in the race with you.

Fear the Lord and listen to him praise you.

Day 25 Journal
#FightBack

_____

_____

_____

_____

_____

_____

_____

_____

_____

_____

_____

_____

_____

_____

_____

_____

_____

_____

_____

_____

_____

_____

_____

Day 26 - You Are a Crown

Today's Date:

You are a crown! Google the words, *beautiful crowns* and then choose which one you think is the most beautiful.

Proverbs 12:4 says, 'A virtuous woman is a crown to her husband: but she that maketh ashamed is as rottenness in his bones.'

Here is what Jonathan Crosby said in his commentary *Let God be True*. "The word crown here is a simple metaphor. A crown honors a person. Kings wear crowns for the honor of their office, and athletes were crowned to honor sporting achievements. A great wife honors her husband by the pleasure and esteem she brings him, and she also crowns his authority by her own submission and that which she requires of her children. A crown is a grand piece of jewelry, and a virtuous woman is a crown to her husband!"

Lol! The commentary said, "...she also crowns his authority by her own submission." We can just end this chapter right now!

Does your husband know that he has authority, or has he been castrated by your lack of honor and submission? You've been praying for him for almost 30 days and that is honorable. But...have you crowned him with your submission or have you rotted his bones?

Crosby says, "What exactly shames a man and rots him from the inside out? A disrespectful and haughty spirit, lack of frequent sex, a dirty or cluttered house, too much talking, a lack of creative sex, running home to mommy and daddy too much, children neglected physically or emotionally, laziness, a negative and complaining attitude, nagging, lack of loyalty, poor manners in public, a critical spirit, a lack of reverence, an out of shape body, insubordination, a prudish approach to sex, self-righteousness, a lack of smiling cheerfulness, correcting details, excessive doting on children, remembering his faults, bristling at correction, that she is disliked by others, and a "I'm just fine as I am" attitude."

Yawl! I'm done! This commentary just broke it all the way down! I hear the voice of John the Baptist… "Repent, for the Kingdom of God is at hand." Wowzers! I guess a man with rotten bones may appreciate the prayer yet the pain from his bones may cause him to not receive the prayer of the one praying.

Let's read a little more from this commentary written by Crosby. He says, "Your husband has likely not told you the truth. If you ask him, he still may not. Consider well. It is hard for a husband to deeply criticize a wife, especially in matters as intimate and personal as marriage and your womanhood. Men also fear the consequences of interrupted domestic tranquility; they resent having to explain the obvious, again; and/or they may not believe it will do any good anyway. He is likely not as pleased as you think."

Today's words will speak more loudly to some than others. If this post has made you feel convicted, just look to the hills and ask forgiveness and then be determined to be a crown! "…she also crowns his authority by her own submission. Submission is a strength NOT a weakness.

Day 26 Journal
#FightBack

Day 27 - Dance Miriam

Today's Date:

Don't let Miriam out praise you.

Exodus 15:20-21 says, 'Then the prophet Miriam, Aaron's sister, took a tambourine in her hand; and all the women went out after her with tambourines and with dancing. And Miriam sang to them: "Sing to the LORD, for he has triumphed gloriously; horse and rider he has thrown into the sea.'

Miriam is the first woman named as a prophet. HUSH! Are you serious? Miriam was a Prophet? I seriously didn't know that! Let's use her as a prototype of the beauty a woman exudes in her authentic praise not fueled by flesh or religion.

Have you ever come outside of your comfort zone to praise God? Have you ever praised like nobody was watching? Have you ever danced before His throne as if every movement spoke of thanks and honor for His grace and mercy? Victory and dancing go together.

Ladies, have you ever been in a marital battle? A marital betrayal, or maybe a porn addiction, drug addiction, gambling addiction, shopping addiction, jealousy within the marriage, bitterness, anger, abuse etc. Did you survive?! Then pick up your tambourine and DANCE MIRIAM!!

Praise God that you survived that battle! (Insert dancing lady emoji with the red dress) Praise God that you are surviving the battle and praise God that you will survive your current battle! Dance! Sing! Praise! Lift your hands!

Sway! Shuffle your feet! Wage war against your opponent the devil and declare victory. Be a Prophet over your situation and dance like Miriam! Lead your sisterhood in a dance of Victory!! Raise you banner! #FightBack

Day 27 Journaling
#FightBack

_____

_____

_____

_____

_____

_____

_____

_____

_____

_____

_____

_____

_____

_____

_____

_____

_____

_____

_____

_____

_____

_____

Day 28 - Honor Your Pasture

Today's Date:

Honor your pasture because you are in it.

Have you ever seen a piece of land covered with grass and other low plants for grazing animals, especially cattle or sheep?

Your pastor works hard during the week to make sure the sheep can graze in the pasture and become full. Take good notes during your next church service. Pray what you learn over your family. If your husband is not serving in a local church, pray that the Lord convicts him. Matthew 9:37 says that, 'The harvest is great, but the workers are few.'

As you have prayed and labored over your husband, know that your pastor prays and labors over you. Just as you have felt frustration over your husband's weaknesses, pastors endure the same thing. Just as you felt like not laboring anymore during the 30 days, your pastor wrestles with having to deal with the sheep, goats and wolves in the pasture.

Your husband's presence in the pasture is needed. His hands on the plow makes things easier for the local pastor to continue to feed the sheep.

Hebrews 13:17 says, 'Obey your [spiritual] leaders and submit to them [recognizing their authority over you], for they are keeping watch over your souls and continually guarding your spiritual welfare as those who will give an account [of their stewardship of you]. Let them do this with joy and not with grief and groans, for this would be of no benefit to you.'

As you have prayed for your husband's protection, promotion, peace of mind, love, courage, leadership, and spiritual growth etc. Pray that he does the same for your pastor. A strong home means a strong church and a strong community. Your pastor needs your husbands love. Hold up the arms of your pastor and buy into the vision of your local church.

Your entire family will be blessed.

Day 28 Journaling
#FightBack

_____

_____

_____

_____

_____

_____

_____

_____

_____

_____

_____

_____

_____

_____

_____

_____

_____

_____

_____

_____

_____

_____

Day 29 - He is Afraid

Today's Date:

He is afraid. Men show fear in less than obvious ways.

Joshua 1:9 says, 'Have I not commanded you? Be strong and courageous. Do not be afraid; do not be discouraged, for the LORD your God will be with you wherever you go.'

Have you ever read that entire chapter? WOW! Read the entire chapter, Joshua is told to *only* be strong and courageous.

Husbands have fears. Fear of rejection, fear of failure, fear of not being able to provide for those he loves, and the list can go on. How does the enemy aggravate your husband? What secret messages does the enemy throw at him to cause fear?

Whatever it is, I pray your husband trusts you enough to expose his fears into the safety of your heart. Why? So that you can pray Joshua 1 into his life. What happens if your husband will not share his fears? Pray and ask God why. There is a reason. Pray that you become that safe place.

Men love to be manly. They were created to be manly. However, there is a little boy in all of them. Are you prudent enough to draw that little boy out and minister to him?

'The heart of her husband trusts in her, and he will not lack anything good.' Do you remember us reading that verse on day 24 from Proverbs 31:11? Feel free to go back to day 24 and refresh your spirit.

Ladies, tap into his fears so that you can speak into his soul. He needs a safe place.

Day 29 Journaling
#FightBack

_____

_____

_____

_____

_____

_____

_____

_____

_____

_____

_____

_____

_____

_____

_____

_____

_____

_____

_____

_____

_____

Day 30 -Well Done

Today's Date:

Well done! (Que streamers and confetti)

We have come to the end of our thirty-day #FightBack challenge. AMAZING! Well done!

Do not stop praying. Some of you have built trust with your husband and stopping now will not be wise. You have created a rhythm and have created momentum. Well done! Keep pressing!

James 5:16 says, 'Confess your faults one to another, and pray one for another, that ye may be healed. The effectual fervent prayer of a righteous man availeth much.'

Being made righteous is a process. Trust the process. Embrace the pain of the crushing. Ohhhh but sisters, do not do it alone! Do not walk through marriage alone. Do not walk out the journey of parenting, or womanhood alone either. It is imperative that you have a safe place to confess your sin, pain, complexities and victories!

Pray for your husband whether you like him or not! Pray for him even if you are headed toward separation or divorce. He is your husband until he is not! Well done!

Day 30 Journaling
#FightBack

Special Instructions from Alaine

Dear Sister girl,

This #FightBack challenge was not designed to complete once and then move on with life. This challenge is designed for you to do over and over and over again. Now that you have completed the challenge, invite some ladies to do it again with you. You can lead them through it. Invite those ladies into your home over something warm to drink (or something cold if it is summertime - lol) and share your experience while doing the challenge. Give them permission to ask you questions because Revelation 12:11 says, 'And they have defeated him by the blood of the Lamb and by their testimony. And they did not love their lives so much that they were afraid to die.'

Lead others into victory. Continue the Titus 2:3-5 ministry. Let us know how things went during your 30 day #FightBack challenge by connecting with us at www.wwmministries.com.

Titus 2 Matters,
Alaine

Acknowledgements

I absolutely could not have done this without my friends and loved ones. I always knew I would write a book but every time I sat down to write it, nothing came. Over the years people told me that they saw me writing a book. Well, here it is, thank you Holy Spirit.

To my husband Gary, thank you for always supporting all the endeavours I have been called to. You never, ever discouraged me but pushed me further than I was comfortable with. I love you.

To my children Isaiah, Hannah, Jeremiah and Gabrielle, you have listened to me dream and talk about everything that concerns me all of your life. Thank you for encouraging me, asking questions and rejoicing with me. At one point in your life I taught you and now you are teaching me. I love you!

Sister Alice Freeman, you are one of a kind. Love. You taught me how to love God, love myself and love others. From 1992 until now, you have spoken life over me. Just when I think I have an idea for one book you speak another deep into the crevices of my soul. There is a library within me. Thank you for lighting my fire. I love you!

Cousin Shawana, you were the first person to read this book after I wrote it. Your feedback and edits filled me with confidence and propelled me to complete the task at hand. Thank you for being patient with me while answering all of my questions, talking me through the publishing process and being a voice of reason. I love you Wan! I'll need you again, stay close.

To Jennifer Faison-Edwards, what can I say? To say that you were a *blessing* to me does not summarize the gratitude I have for you. Your benevolence was supreme. Your expertise, feedback and edits were stellar. Thank you for being everything I needed to get this book to the publisher. I love you!

Gloria Doughty, you copied and pasted this 30-day challenge that started out on Facebook into a Word document, wrapped it and told me to write the book. I was shaken. I was propelled and I am grateful. Thank you so much for your obedience. I love you!

Lastly, to the ladies that are always listening to me talk about my long and short-term goals; Nicole Bauer, Victoria Artis, and Kimberly Gagliano you were right there beside me giving me ideas for the cover of this book. Thank you, for helping me explore the design. I love each of you, deeply!

References

1. *"H2896 - towb - Strong's Hebrew Lexicon (KJV)." Blue Letter Bible. Web. 3 Sep, 2018. <https://www.blueletterbible.org//lang/lexicon/lexicon.cfm?Strongs=H2896&t=KJV>.*
2. 'Irritation.' Merriam-Webster. 2019. Web. 3 September 2019. **https://www.merriam-webster.com/dictionary/noun**
3. 'Irritation.' Merriam-Webster. 2019. Web. 3 September 2019. **https://www.merriam-webster.com/thesaurus/irritation**
4. 'Restitution' Merriam-Webster. 2019. Web. 1 January 2019. **https://www.merriam-webster.com/dictionary/restitution**
5. James Glentworth Butler. The Bible-work: The Old Testament, Volume 6. New York: Funk & Wagnalls, 1892.print

Additional Notes

Additional Notes